ABOUT THE AUTHOR

Judy Bartkowiak is a life coach specialising in working with parents and children in the UK using Neuro Linguistic Programming.

Judy has written a number of NLP books and is the author of Teach Yourself: Be a happier parent with NLP (Hodder Education).

Included in the book is input from Jeanette Wallis who specialises in using NLP with mums-to-be and new mums (contact details at the end of the book).

Judy and Jeanette believe passionately in NLP which they were introduced to by Sue Knight, author of several NLP books and a world class NLP Trainer.

CONTENTS

INTRODUCTION

NLP is a completely different way of viewing your world. Once you have been introduced to the NLP way of thinking and communicating it will seem like you've come home. It is respectful of others and more importantly of yourself and it is positive.

John Grinder and Richard Bandler developed what they came to call NLP from a combination of Virginia Satir's Family Therapy, Franz Perls' Gestalt Therapy and the work of Milton Erickson in the area of language patterns. What Grinder and Bandler added was the idea of coding excellence by observing how effective people communicated and forming ground rules that would bring these results to anyone who applied them. These ground rules are what we call NLP or Neuro Linguistic Programming.

This workbook is designed first and foremost to be a practical workbook for you to use, write in and apply on a day to day basis.

Other NLP workbooks available are:

NLP for Children

NLP for Teens

NLP for Parents

NLP for Teachers

NLP Back to Work

NLP Sports, Exercise and Fitness

THE GROUND RULES

Neuro Linguistic Programming has a number of presuppositions or ground rules that personally, I have found life changing. I hope you do too.

Read through them before you start reading the book because they underpin all the tools and techniques covered in the different chapters.

I have written the ground rules specifically for you to apply to your own life so make notes in the book and fill in the little quizzes and lists so you can really engage with NLP.

1) If you always do what you've always done

then you will always get what you've always got

How often do we repeat the same self talk or behaviour pattern and get something we don't want? Perhaps we tell ourselves that next time things will be different; we will do or say something different. Yet given the same circumstances next time we repeat the same pattern and get the same result.

If you want a different result, a positive outcome, then you need to change what you are doing and your self-talk.

It's no good thinking that suddenly out of the blue by doing the same thing every time you will one day get a different result because you won't.

You also won't get a different result by getting someone else to change what they do.

We do what we do because of our beliefs and values, our experiences of life and our cultural environment.

When we make a change at one level it impacts on the next level so in order to change at the behavioural level, you need to consider the other levels of change. We will explore this in detail in the chapter on identity where we will consider the NLP 'Logical Levels of Change Model'.

We sometimes hold on to beliefs from our childhood even though they may be limiting our choices of behaviour. Later on in the book we will revisit them and get rid of those that don't serve us well in our life today.

Examples of limiting beliefs are the voices in your head from your parents or teachers saying things like 'Do what the Doctor says because they know what they're talking about' or 'she has a problem with maths.'

2) You have the resources to do whatever you want to do

What an inspiring idea! Imagine living your life as if you already have all the skills you need?

Just the other day I was treating a teenager who was struggling at school. He told me he couldn't be bothered, couldn't concentrate, wanted to mess about and wanted to leave school because it was so boring and pointless.

What were the skills he thought he lacked?

- *The ability to be bothered*
- *To concentrate*
- *Focus*
- *Be engaged*

So we talked some more and soon found that he had all those skills already because he would apply himself to a new video game and play it solidly for three days working up the levels until he had successfully completed it.

Nat was amazed and he was able to identify the structure of the skill (how he did it – the process) and the underlying belief that it was important, a challenge and gave him a competitive edge over his mates.

So we anchored these skills and now he is using the anchor at school for the skills he already had somewhere else.

You too have a huge resource of skills that you have been building since childhood and each one enables you to apply it in different ways by transferring it to the application you need it for.

What are the skills you need now for your life as a new mum or a pregnant mum? We will look at skills later in the book in the chapter on identity. For now, believe you have all the skills you need and be curious about where they are.

3) *If someone else can do it you can too*

You can also acquire new skills and hone existing ones by modelling (or copying) them in someone who demonstrates that skill really well. This is such a reassuring belief to take on when you are a new mum, isn't it?

How many of us struggle and tell ourselves 'I can't do this' or 'I'm not cut out to be a mum'? We all have difficult days when every mum you meet seems to be coping better than us. If they can do it, we can do it. What's the skill? Be observant and find the skill they are using and then find it in you and use it too.

We all have the skill to model or copy and just as you can pick up a skill from someone else; your baby is picking them up from you. We can use this to our advantage to pass on the skills we want them to have in life. We are models for our baby.

We can also be models for ourselves. Are you different with certain friends or family? Do you behave differently at work? You can model the 'you' in one place and use that 'you' where you need it now.

The skills we had at work such as being assertive and making decisions can easily escape us during pregnancy and during those exhausting early months with a new baby. You <u>do</u> have them and I will introduce you to the NLP Time Line where you can find them again and put them back into practice.

4) There is no failure only feedback

Failure is a common emotion for new mums. After all the focus on us during pregnancy and then the birth, suddenly everyone's only interested in the baby.

If every time you toppled over as a child learning to walk, you gave up because you felt a failure, you'd still be crawling today!

Similarly, scientists spend years repeating their experiments changing single elements each time. They do not consider each one to be a failure but simply another way that it doesn't work. Each one is a learning experience.

You love your baby, of course you do but it's very demanding. Night and day 24/7 you are on call. Your baby cries so you run through all the possibilities, hungry, nappy needs changing, tired, not tired, wind and so on.

Wouldn't it be easier if they had a digital print out on their forehead telling an exhausted mum what baby needs?

Most of us feel we've failed when baby is crying because we feel that instinctively we should know what they need.

However, this is not so. Baby crying is feedback and although we need to work out what baby needs, it is our choice whether we want to take the feedback as failure or simply a learning opportunity.

Lots of new mums feel guilty about being annoyed with their baby, leaving it with someone when they go out or feeling that they are 'not a good mother'. We can reframe this as 'regret' and we can disassociate. This means imagining what someone else would think if they were a 'fly on the wall'. They probably wouldn't judge as harshly as we judge ourselves. Guilt is a choice and I have a great exercise to tackle this later in the book.

5) *If you spot it you've got it*

When you notice a quality (or a failing) in someone else this is because in some way you have it too which is why you can recognise it.

This is because we each process our world differently and notice different things. So if you notice something about someone else, they are probably noticing the same thing about you.

We tend to be attracted to people like us with similar values and beliefs which make it more likely that you will notice similarities amongst the mums you socialise with. When you notice a quality in one of them ask yourself 'how am I like this too?'

6) If you try, you won't succeed

How often do we say 'I'll try and get the baby to sleep'? Do we 'try to breastfeed'?

When we use the word 'try' we cover our backs in case we don't succeed. If anyone should point a finger then we are OK because we only said we would 'try'.

Are you 'trying for a baby'?

There are lots of medical reasons for women to have a history of miscarriage. In Jeanette Wallis's practice (www.wallshealth.co.uk) she sees a proportion of women whose belief is that their body has let them down. In that group once she has facilitated them to change their negative belief to feel better about themselves, they go to full term.

Where you put your focus is what you get.

The trouble is that our subconscious mind knows that we are only trying so we don't put much effort into it because we have programmed ourselves to only 'try'.

Do you ask your partner to 'try' to get the baby to sleep or 'try' to remember to pick up some nappies on the way home? How hard will they 'try'?

Are you 'trying to be a good mum'? You are the best mum for your baby because you are the mum. Trust your intuitions, they are usually right.

If you really do want something then DO IT!

7) *The map is not the territory*

We receive a huge number of inputs at any time yet our conscious mind can only process about 7 of them. Of course we don't each process the same 7 so how you see the world is different from how others see it.

What we notice is based on our environment, experiences, values and beliefs which make up our identity.

Your own map has changed beyond recognition. Here's a way to realise just how much.

<u>Exercise</u>

Write a letter to **your past-self**. Write a letter to yourself on the night before you had your child. What would you tell yourself? What would you need to hear?

Dear ....

Our babies have their own map and if we want to understand them we need to enter their territory by stepping into their 'shoes' and seeing it from their viewpoint.

Another map you may want to explore is your partners because whilst you are experiencing a life changing event, so are they and they too will be challenged by limiting beliefs and lack of confidence. Unlike you, they may not have the words or the friendships within which to express them.

Many pregnant mums fear how having a baby will affect their relationship and understanding each other's very different maps will keep your relationship strong.

8) The mind and body are interlinked and affect each other

If you've just had a baby or are pregnant or perhaps wanting to get pregnant you will be very aware of how the mind and body are interlinked.

Jeanette sees many women with breech presentation. She told me that often they are career women who are used to being in control and generally left work late in the pregnancy. The unborn child senses this. The mum-to-be can be so disassociated with the baby that it literally stands on its own two feet!

Once they are assisted to relax and re-associate with the baby, the baby turns.

The following experiments will show you just how powerful your mind is in controlling your body. It may be easier if you ask your partner or a friend to read out the instructions while you do the exercise.

A)

1) Stand and put your right arm straight out in
   front of you with your finger pointing.

2) Remain facing forwards and move your arm
   as far around to the side and if you can,
   behind you, keeping your arm straight.
   Notice the point you reach with your finger.
   What are you pointing at?

3) Now close your eyes and repeat the exercise
   and this time visualise (imagine) going
   further round, staying relaxed and
   comfortable.

4) Now imagine getting another few inches further, again stay relaxed and comfortable.

5) And another few inches again staying relaxed and comfortable.

6) Now another few inches.

7) Open your eyes and see how much further you have managed to reach when you use the power of your mind.

B)

1) Put out your right arm, palm down

2) Your partner rests his hand lightly on your arm. He doesn't need to push on it, just enough pressure to give you something to push against.

3) Test it by pushing your arm up and notice the effort it takes.

4) Now think of something that hasn't gone well for you recently. Think about it as if it's happening now. Then raise your arm and notice how much harder it is to push your partner's hand up.

5) Break state for a moment by shaking your arm and then return to holding it out again with your partner's hand on it as before.

6) Now think of something that's gone really well recently and think of it as if it's happening now. Then raise your arm again and notice how much easier it is to push your partner's hand up.

By using your mind, you can influence your body. Athletes and sportsmen do this all the time.

We use this concept when we anchor positive feelings, feelings of being calm and in control and being brave. We will learn how to anchor later in the book p75 and you can use it during pregnancy, in labour and as a new mum.

9) Mind the gap

This is such an important one for new mums isn't it? How often do we react spontaneously and emotionally rather than take a step back and be objective?

This could be responding to something the doctor or midwife has said, your boss, your partner, your mum? Our hormones are in turmoil and we are experiencing the most major change in our lives. We have 100% responsibility for a completely dependent human life and we are totally exhausted.

Before responding, stop and consider how an impartial bystander might see or hear the situation differently. This is called 'disassociating' and it separates us from the emotion of the situation so we can decide what options we have.

You will find this really helpful as your baby heads towards the toddler stage!

10) The person with the most flexibility controls
the system

Flexibility enables us to choose between different options regarding how we respond in both our internal self talk and what we say and do. The more options we have, the more chance we will be in rapport with those around us and can therefore influence them.

One of the great ways to use this flexibility is to be solution focussed rather than problem focussed. Some pregnant mums worry about the birth, have nightmares that they will end up giving birth in the car or a corridor in the hospital, that they will be induced or that things will go wrong.

You have the choice to visualise positively, visualise things going well and focussing on your desirable outcome rather than looking for problems. When you are flexible and make positive choices the outcome is good because that's where you are putting your attention.

CHAPTER 1: IDENTITY AND SELF ESTEEM

I think becoming a mum is probably the biggest life changing event you can experience, not just for you but for your partner as well. It can be life changing too for your own parents as they face the fact of you now being a parent yourself. At such a time you need to spend some time considering your identity.

Let's look at the Logical Levels of Change. Have a look at the diagram on the next page. We start at the bottom of the pyramid at our environment and work up towards our purpose in life at the top. It's a great way to harmonise our identity by looking at what underpins it and what it means in terms of our direction and goals in life.

Purpose
Who you
want to be

Identity
Who you are

Beliefs and Values
Why you do it

Skills
How you do it

Behaviour
What you do

Environment
Where you do what you do

Environment

Think about where you live, work and the cultures of those places. How does your environment affect you?

What could you change about it that would make it work better for you when you are a new mum with a baby?

We tend to get very focussed on buying baby equipment and decorating the nursery but the biggest problem new mums experience can be isolation from other adults.

Now may be a good time to take up an activity that you can continue after the baby is born that will enable you to mix with adults and do something for yourself.

Most mums find their ante natal group or NCT group a real life-saver but doing something you enjoy such as joining a book group, tennis club or a gym will also give you something for yourself.

Does your current employer offer part time work or 'work from home' flexibility? Have you considered retraining or setting up your own company? I have another book in this series entitled NLP Back to Work that gives you lots of ideas about earning money without working full time.

Does your partner know what to expect and have you discussed how to manage the logistics of caring for the baby, work, household chores and time for yourselves?

You may want to revisit your environment once you've been up the Logical levels to your identity.

Behaviour

If you always do what you've always done you will always get what you've always got. If you are not happy with the outcomes, change your behaviour because you can't control other people's behaviour, not even your baby's.

Write down what you do. It may be easiest to focus on a particular day such as yesterday. Write down everything you did. Then tick whether it has value to you as a person. If it doesn't you may want to consider dumping it or delegating it.

What I did	Did it have value for me

Clearly there will be things on the list that may not add value to your life as a person (such as nappy changing!) but they may fulfil your belief about what a good mother should be in which case they are of value to you.

Skills

What are your skills? What are you good at? What did you used to be good at? Use the exercise on Time Lines on p36 to revisit them and bring them to the present.

Do this by identifying the skill you need and going back along the Time Line to find it. Anchor it using the anchoring exercise and then go back to the point on the Time Line representing today in order to put that skill into practise where you need it now.

A skill can be anything from being able to put on lipstick without a mirror or doing a cartwheel to being able to manage a meeting.

What do you do well?

Here's an exercise to help you bring these to mind.

Exercise

Write down all the things you can do on the left hand side of the page. Then write alongside each one, what that means in terms of your being a new mother. For example, if you can tell a joke it means you can hold your baby's attention. Look at each skill you have in your repertoire and ask yourself 'What does that also mean I can do?'

What I can do   *What that means*

Have you impressed yourself?

Let's take this a step further now. We often overlook the things we are good at because we hardly notice them. Our friends do though! So do our family and our partner.

Go back to the list on the previous page and add to it all those things that other people say you do well. Ask your partner, ask your friends! Don't make any comment afterwards though, just note it down.
Then complete the right hand side of the page with what that means for you as a mother.

Taking it on a further stage; what have you noticed that other mums do well? I expect you do that well too, that's why you've noticed it so add those things to your list which hopefully by now is really long!

You can add to that list at any time by asking yourself, when things aren't going so well:

- o What skill do I need?
- o When did I have that skill?
- o What did I believe about myself or what was my self-talk that enabled me to use that skill?
- o Now take on that belief in order to access the skill.......and add it to your list!

Believing in yourself and your skills is using your strengths from one area of your life to enhance another. During pregnancy you will need to be assertive and make decisions. Use the Time Line to help you find this resource in your past.

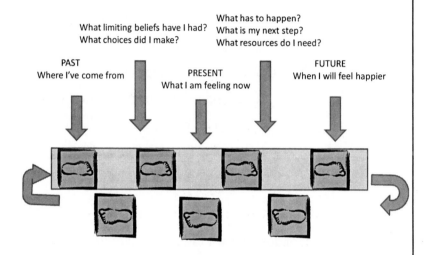

Imagine a line on the floor stretching out in front of you. It will represent time. At one end is your childhood and at the other end is old age. Stand on the line at a point that represents today, the present.

- Think about you today, how you're feeling, what you're doing, who you're with and what's good about now.

- Look forward into the future and go and stand on the point that represents when you will feel confident as a mother.
- One of two things has happened.
  - You went straight to the point and are standing on it
  - You couldn't move or are dithering, not sure when it could be

Think about this vision of you being confident, how it feels, what you're doing and who is there, what you can see and hear and feel. Enjoy this great experience of your vision.

- If you are still at today's point you need to think about why you can't visualise it. Think about what you need in order to move forward. What skills do you need? When you know what you need, think about where in your life you have that resource.

It is a strong NLP belief that we all have the resources we need for whatever we want to do. Sometimes the resource is one we use in another part of our life and don't realise can be applied to this situation where we need it now.

If for example it is confidence you need to ask yourself where you have confidence or when you had it.

- Go to that point on the time line when you had the skill you need and really 'associate into it' recall every aspect of that feeling. When it feels strong, anchor it (p75)by making an action such as squeezing your earlobe. We will cover anchoring in more detail later.
- Now move back to today with that anchor for the skill and enjoy the feeling.

Use the time line to move forwards and back along the line exploring your feelings at each point. If you are visual and tend to think in images then focus on the images at each point. If you are more auditory and focus more on what is said, then imagine what you can hear. If you are kinaesthetic and focus more on feelings then do that at each point.

Beliefs

What beliefs do you hold about being a mother?

Beliefs are what we hold to be true at any point in time. They change as we learn more about life and meet new people, visit new places and read more about the world. Having a baby will probably have changed some of your beliefs and this can present challenges for you as a new mum.

Let's take a moment to examine your beliefs about being a mum now.

<u>I believe I am a good mother when I</u> ....

You may also hold beliefs that don't serve you well. These are called 'limiting beliefs'. They are often 'hang overs' from our own parents and the beliefs they passed onto us. They may have been workable then but are they good for you in the environment you are in today?

Changing beliefs is quite natural, just like we grow out of believing in Father Christmas!

Write a list of the limiting beliefs you hold. If they don't come readily to mind, ask your partner and friends what beliefs they think you hold that are not very useful to you right now.

Here is my list of limiting beliefs.

Now pick the most inconvenient and limiting of them and we are going to work together to get rid of it but first we have to find out what positive intention it has. This is because we hold onto beliefs sometimes because although they might limit our choices in life, we subconsciously quite like that.

For example; I have a friend who 'can't drive at night' which limits her but mostly enables her to get lifts to parties. If she got rid of this limiting belief she'd have to drive and therefore not be able to drink! There is definitely a pay-off for her limiting belief.

In this next exercise we are going to disassociate from the belief. That means to inspect the belief as if it was a separate part of you and question it.

Here's how we do that. It's called 'perceptual positioning' in NLP. Arrange three chairs as in the diagram.

Position 1 is you. Position 2 is the limiting belief and Position 3 is the impartial observer. Establish three positions or places in a triangle like this.

Position 3

(impartial observer)

X

X   X

Position 1   Position 2

(you)   (your limiting belief)

Stand at position 1 and say what gets in the way of what you want to do, identify that limiting belief.

Break state by giving yourself a little shake to change your mood.

Now go to position 2 and imagine you are that limiting belief and tell position 1 about your positive intention.

Go back to Position 1 and respond to this. Then return to Position 2 if you feel the limiting belief has more to say.

When all's said; break state again and go to position 3 to comment on what you have heard from positions 1 and 2 as if you were someone passing by and hearing them talk. How do you feel the situation could be resolved?

Now without breaking state, return to position 1 and say what you feel about the limiting belief now.

There are lots of ways you can use perceptual positioning. If you have an area of conflict in your life you can make Position 2 the other person or the area of conflict. It's a great way of stepping into someone else's shoes and exploring their map of the world.

<u>Values</u>

The values you hold are unlikely to change. These are the values you were brought up with and will pass on to your own children. Many of them will be part of your culture or environment.

What values do you hold about being or becoming a parent? If you aren't living according to your values you will have a sense of disharmony. To correct this you will need to make changes to your beliefs, behaviour or environment because each level underpins the next.

<u>What I value about being a mother is.....</u>

Identity

This is who you <u>are</u> not the role you play at home or at work but the essential <u>you</u>. Who are you?

Exercise

A good way to think about this is to write down how other people would describe you. Imagine you are one of your friends or colleagues and 'disassociate', see yourself as others see you. We tend to be very self critical and judge ourselves severely, seeing the best in others rather than in ourselves.

It's helpful to ask them as well. When you do that, just ask and write down or remember what they say but make no comment. Write a list and leave a space underneath each one so we can write something else down in a minute.

My friends would describe me as............

Link these qualities to your new identity as a mother
or mother-to-be by asking of each one 'How will I
apply this in my life as a mother?' and write that
down underneath each one.

Now that you are feeling good about yourself and have banished any unhelpful limiting beliefs about yourself; this is a good time to do a 'Circle of Excellence' exercise which you can use when you need to feel fantastic.

<u>Exercise</u>

- Imagine a circle drawn on the floor or if you prefer use a mat. This is your circle of excellence.
- Step into it and think of all these great things your friends would say about you, think of things you have done that you are proud of and really associate into the good images, sounds and feelings that you experience in the circle.
- Use the anchoring exercise here to anchor this and you can use it whenever you need it.

Purpose

This is at the top of the logical levels and refers to why we are here, which is a big question. It may be one that has changed for you since becoming a parent and it affects all the logical levels so if you feel your purpose has changed, how does that affect your identity, values and beliefs, skills, behaviour and environment?

Parenthood is a time of change and it affects us in so many ways. It is important to take time to work through the levels and put them into harmony one with another.

<u>CHAPTER 2: GETTING WHAT YOU WANT</u>

In order to get what you want, whether that is the home you want, a job or the lifestyle you want with your new baby, you need to understand about rapport.

Instinctively we know when we are in rapport, like the two ladies above, we find ourselves walking in step and almost finishing each other's sentences. We might make some physical contact and even begin to look like each other.

During pregnancy and birth you will have met new people; new mums like yourself, health care professionals, maybe new neighbours if you've moved to a bigger house and new colleagues if you've changed jobs. It is therefore really important to know how to gain rapport with people who aren't your friends.

First we need to know how we 'tick' how we process the world around us. When we understand how we operate, we can work out how others process which means we can match it to get rapport. In rapport, we can then influence the outcome because we will both be speaking the 'same language'.

In NLP there are 3 languages or 'internal representations', visual, auditory and kinaesthetic. Although we may use each of these at different times, we will prefer one and we use that most of the time.

Visual

You think in pictures and images, using expressions like 'do you see what I mean' or 'look at it from my point of view'. Your descriptions will have colour and texture. Views and your surroundings will be important to you as will your appearance. You will be more aware of the change in your figure during pregnancy and be anxious to lose the weight afterwards so you can get back into your favourite clothes.

If you are visual, how you and your baby look will be important as will their nursery and baby equipment. If your surroundings don't look nice this may upset you more than most.

You may want to write down what healthcare professionals say to you because your memory for what's said to you may not be as good as your visual memory.

Auditory

You are auditory if you enjoy music, notice the sounds around you and prefer your friends to call rather than text or email. You tend to remember what people say to you or what you've heard on the radio better than what you've read. You will find the sound of a baby crying or children shouting more disturbing than other mums.

You might use expressions like 'did you hear what I said?' or 'please be quiet'.

54

Kinaesthetic

You are an active person and enjoy being on the go. Exercise and fitness is important to you and you like to have physical contact with your friends and your family. You notice the temperature and feel uncomfortable if it's not right. You may find the physical experience of being pregnant and the birth more upsetting than other mums so keep up your exercise routines especially those that are not weight bearing such as cycling and swimming. Join a gym with a crèche and explore other exercise options you can do with baby.

You may use expressions like 'let's get going' or 'that doesn't feel right' because you are very sensitive to atmosphere.

Another layer of rapport is called 'Meta programmes' and are more about personality.

Meta Programmes

Read through all of these to discover which Meta programmes apply most to you and those you spend time with. By matching their Meta programme you can have rapport and influence.

Big chunk/small chunk

No this isn't about chocolate!

If you are 'big chunk' you will think broad brush in concepts rather than detail. You will perhaps be thinking about 'motherhood' as a concept rather than a 'small chunk' mother who has all the details worked out.

You probably didn't want a lot of detailed instructions on pregnancy, how to prepare for the birth or wean baby but just wanted the rough ideas so you could work out the rest yourself.

If you enjoy detail you will be 'small chunk'. You will be interested in the detailed information about every aspect of your new baby and check out books and websites so you have everything you want to know.

If you are one and your partner is the other then that is an ideal combination to ensure that between you, you have the detailed information you may need.

Choices/Process

A 'choices' mum is one who likes options and a 'process' or 'procedures' mum prefer to have a plan of action, a list and work through it.

If you are choices you will have spent some time considering all the options for your birth plan and weighing them up, talking to other mums and healthcare professionals. You enjoy this choosing time and will spend time choosing baby equipment, decoration for the nursery and baby clothes.

If you are 'process' you'll just work through a list and possibly find choices annoying. You may want to save time by using comparison charts where the research work has already been done.

Towards/Away from

'Towards' mums have things they want to do, they have plans and ideas, goals to meet and tend to be achievement orientated. They will set their mind to getting what they want and won't think about the consequences of failure.

By contrast, the 'away from' mum fears failure and expends energy in avoiding things. If you are 'away from' you will be more of a worrier because you will be problem focussed.

You will probably have invested in a cot mattress to monitor heart beat and baby monitor with video screen. If this is you then switch your self-talk to focussing on what you <u>do</u> want. For example if you find yourself worrying about your pregnancy or your baby, instead talk about what you want to be like and how you want your baby to be.

Internally/externally referenced

An internally referenced mum does things because they want to do them and because they meet their own goals and values. They won't be swayed by others and will live their life the way they want rather than referring to others.

An externally focused mum will be influenced by others and rarely check in with what they want for themselves. If this is you then just check in from time to time with your own values by asking yourself 'and what do I want?'

Match/Mismatch

Some mums will notice what they have in common with other mums and some notice what is different. You can instantly tell a mismatch person because they tend to contradict you!

Mums do tend to match quite a bit in order to build rapport and the shared experience of pregnancy and birth will encourage this.

Associated/Disassociated

An 'associated' mum will be more emotional and sensitive, take things to heart and be anxious to please. You will get disheartened if things aren't going well and take it quite personally.

A 'disassociated' mum will be slightly more distant and be able to get things into perspective without getting upset by pitfalls. You will cope with the emotional rollercoaster of early motherhood better than the associated mum because you can separate your emotions from the situation.

How do we use this?

Once you know what you are you can easily match with those you meet by using the same words and expressions as them so they understand you. It's as easy as that!

You can achieve even better rapport by matching their body language, facial expressions and their tone of voice. It may seem strange at first but they don't notice when you match if you do it well.

You can even match with baby as they mimic you quite naturally. You can build rapport with your baby even before she is born. They are naturally in tune with you and sense your mood, hear the music you play and how you walk.

If you want to take the lead and use this for getting them to sleep you match them for a while to establish rapport and then start making your own actions for them to copy such as going to sleep. I'll go through this in the modelling chapter.

Barriers to rapport

Rapport breaks down when you use what we call deletions, distortions and generalisations. Be aware of these especially in situations where you need to communicate accurately, for example to health care professionals.

- Deletions are when you give vague descriptions such as 'I feel bad' or 'she isn't feeding'. Instead be ready with a diary of what has been happening and what exact symptoms or behaviour you have observed. You may even find there is a pattern that enables you to find your own solution.

- Distortions are when you say what you imagine someone to be thinking or what you think will happen in the future such as 'I expect you think I'm stupid' or 'I know what you're going to say'. It's better to say what you want to say and then check out with them.

- Generalisations are when you use words like 'always' and 'never' and 'everyone'. Focus on the facts and what you feel now, the patterns you have observed and notice, in particular the exceptions. For example, 'I keep getting headaches at night but I've noticed that I don't get headaches if I go to bed late' rather than 'I always get a headache at night'.

- The word **'don't'** is what NLP calls an embedded command. We tend to respond best when we are told 'what to do' not 'what not to do'. Focus on what you <u>do</u> want. If you are instructing a babysitter or even your partner, tell them what you do want rather than 'Don't forget to....' say 'remember to.....' instead.

Rapport is about communicating and you cannot 'not communicate' because we do it all the time both verbally and non-verbally with everyone we meet and over these months you will meet many new people with whom it will be very important to have rapport.

When you match the other person's internal representation and Meta programmes you can tell them what you want and because you are in rapport you will get a favourable response because they will want to stay in rapport with you.

Many pregnant and new mums worry about how the relationship with their partner will change once they have their baby. By practising rapport and teaching it to your partner you will be able to build rapport and understanding for your life as parents. Then you can teach it to your children!

<u>CHAPTER 3: MODELLING</u>

Modelling is the copying of a skill you observe in someone else that you want for yourself and modelling a skill you want someone else to copy. This could be very useful to you as you go through the life changing experience of pregnancy and birth. You may meet mums who have a skill you'd like to copy and you can model your own skills from other areas in your life or from your past life and then you will want to model skills that you want your baby to copy.

This modelling technique is unique to NLP and personally I find it really empowering to believe that I can pinch other people's best bits and have them for myself!

Here's how to do it:

- Observe the skill
- Be specific about what part of it you want
- Find several models of excellence of it
- Notice the structure, how they do it step by step
- Extract the underlying belief about the ability to do it
- Practise it yourself
- Incorporate it into your repertoire of skills

A skill can be as small as simply a facial expression or gesture, a sports skill, how someone holds their baby, anything that you admire in someone else. Be curious about the skill and notice every aspect of it. Look at when they do it, how they do it and what comes first, second, third and so on. You can even model celebrities, film stars, anyone! So you can do this on the TV, watching a movie, at work anywhere.

Identify the exact nature of the skill. It's much easier to model something specific rather than something vague. For example you might admire the way someone 'puts their baby to sleep' or 'plays with their baby' but that is too vague and there are many skills involved in each of these. You need to break down what you have observed into small parts and identify exactly what these are. Which skill precisely do you need?

Find examples of excellence for that precise skill. It could be that those who do that particular skill with excellence don't use it in the way you intend to use it but for the purposes of modelling this doesn't matter. Spend time watching those with the skill and note down everything you observe. Practise whenever you can and be curious about the response you get.

Some of your models will be easier to approach than others but with those who you feel confident with, ask them how they do the thing you are observing.

You can be specific, 'I've noticed how you are very good at getting Sophie to take her bottle, how do you do that?'It is not unusual for people not to know how they do something they do well because they do it quite naturally.

You need to dig deeper and ask about their underlying beliefs. If we use the analogy of the potter it may help to explain why this is important. If you are watching a potter mould a lump of clay you can guess what he is making and you can copy what he does but you will only make the same thing as the potter if you know what the potter is imagining in his head about what form the clay will take.

Ask 'I've noticed how Joe seems to eat everything. How do you do that? What do you say to yourself just before you feed him?'Here we have found the skill in our personal life and a model who you can ask about underlying beliefs.

Once you have the underlying belief or indeed several from different models, match their belief about this skill with your own. You need to acquire the belief. First you need to examine your belief and where it comes from. Maybe it is from childhood and no longer useful to you in your current environment or in the workplace. When parents pass on beliefs to children they are not necessarily thinking about the future.

Beliefs are not values, they can be changed as we gather new information and experiences. Re-examine your limiting beliefs because it may be restricting your options.

You can model any skill you want whether that be in a sports and fitness situation, personally or work related. Once you have the structure and the belief you have the skill.

Use this space to write down what skills you've observed in your friends or colleagues that you'd like to have for yourself.

I want this skill   *From*

Now write down below what you could pass on to them.

Believe it or not you can even use modelling to get your baby to sleep. This time you want baby to model you.

Babies watch what you do from the moment they are born and they want to copy you. This is how they learn and develop the socialising skills they will need in life. They are so in tune with you that they will pick up on your moods and copy your mannerisms and facial expressions.

We've all experienced those times when exasperated or just incredibly tired, we pass baby to someone else and baby's mood changes. From being fractious they suddenly seem more relaxed. This is because they have picked up on our mood.

We can use this to our advantage but rarely do. Here's how to do it. Put your baby where you want her to sleep but somewhere where she can see you when you lie down. A good place is by the sofa or by your bed in her cot or basket.

Turn down the lighting and put some quiet music on. I like to use classical music but choose something she won't associate with singing along to because you want the music to be in the background.

Now spend some time facing your baby and get her attention. Start by copying what she does, mirror her. Avoid mirroring any crying but you can copy any hand movements and head movements. This is called matching and mirroring. At the moment she is taking the lead, you are copying her. After a while she will be intrigued by this and engage with the activity. Make your movements quite clear and definite so she can see you are copying what she does.

Now you need to take the lead. Start to make quiet noises or clap your hands gently, tap your nose and get her watching everything you do. You need to get her to mirror your behaviour now.

It may take some time especially if she is crying when you start but as long as you know she is fed and changed, she should be ready for a sleep.

Once she is mirroring and matching your behaviour you can start the sleepy routine. Yawn very obviously and say things like 'Mummy's tired', 'Mummy's going to sleep now' and lie down so she can see you. Now it's important that you don't get up because she needs to be lying down as well. If you sit up again, she won't settle because she's now expecting you to do something else that she can copy so turn your phone off and really focus on going to sleep (even if you're actually dressed to go out and the babysitter is due any minute!).

Modelling is a great skill as it means you can be whatever you choose to be and model for others what you want them to acquire from you. Apply it to every part of your life as ongoing personal development.

CHAPTER 4: STATE MANAGEMENT

As you prepare for motherhood, during pregnancy and in the early months after the birth there will be times when you feel tired, frustrated and wonder whether you've made a mistake and yet there will be other times when you feel on top of the world.

During pregnancy there are many times when you need to be assertive or you need to make decisions. For example when you are talking to healthcare professionals about the sort of birth you want or speaking to the doctor about your baby. We used to have a voice and be able to make decisions didn't we but where has it gone now?

You can use anchoring in combination with the Time Line exercise to go back in time to when you had a voice and were able to make decisions, anchor it and use it now.

Anchoring is a core NLP technique that gives us the ability to access or recall a good feeling whenever you need it by making an action that reminds you of it.

You probably already have subconscious anchors. For example, maybe the sight of your sleeping baby gives you a lovely warm feeling of pride and love.

This is a positive subconscious anchor. Maybe baby crying is a negative subconscious anchor. By making our anchor conscious we can actively use it to give us some control over our state.

First though you need to link the action with the memory so that it works when you need it to.

A common anchor action is to put your thumb and first finger together to form a circle like this.

Decide what your anchor or trigger will be and practise it a few times so it comes quite naturally when you need it.

Here's the anchoring process

- Find somewhere quiet and close your eyes.
- Think about a time when you felt completely happy, totally optimistic, confident and able to cope with anything. This could be some time in the past. Choose a really good example of that feeling.
- Make the images very clear and sharp, give them colour and contrast and make them bright as if the light is shining on them. Focus on you in the picture and give your

image some detail so you are the star of the show.

- Where are you, give the scene a backdrop and context?
- What are you saying and what conversations can you hear?
- What do you feel? Are you hot or cold, what feelings can you sense around you and what are you feeling now. Where in your body is the feeling situated, put your hand where the feeling is located.
- Now use your anchor.
- When the feelings and images diminish release your anchor and break state by thinking of something completely different for a moment.
- Then repeat the exercise until it comes naturally and will be accessible whenever you need it.

You can use your anchor throughout your pregnancy, during the birth and at stressful times in the early months.

You can anchor feelings of happiness, confidence, resourcefulness and focus, anything in fact. You can use it outside of family life, at work and in your sport.

Some people find that wearing a particular piece of clothing or jewellery acts as a good anchor. They put it on and because they have established it as an anchor in an exercise like the one just described, they immediately feel strong or brave, focussed or whatever they have decided.

Children have anchors such as their comfort blanket, favourite teddy bear or doll. You will be their anchor in the early years but if they have an anchor that they can access without you or without a physical object they will be more resourceful because the anchor is not dependent on something else, only them.

Another technique you can use to control your mood or state is called SWISH.

<u>Exercise</u>

First identify the trigger to your bad mood or 'unresourceful state' as we would call it in NLP.

What sets it off? Is it something you see (if you are visual), something you hear (auditory) or something you feel (kinaesthetic)?

Make that negative image really powerful in your mind, focus on it and put it on a big screen as if you're in a cinema watching yourself react negatively to the trigger. Like this.

Now break state by thinking about something else for a moment.

Next, think about how you'd like to react to that trigger. Maybe you want to be calm and in control, be smiling or simply not bothered by it.

Imagine what that would look, sound and feel like and make an image of you like that. Put that image in the bottom left hand corner of the screen you imagined earlier. Like this.

Now say SWISH to yourself and make an action like swatting a fly away from your face and as you do that, make the images swap around so the positive one is the main image and the negative one is small and in the corner. Like this.

Practise it several times until you can just say SWISH (auditory) do the action (kinaesthetic), or see the positive image (visual) in order to get the changed mood.

You can teach this to your toddler. I've used this with children who claim not to like vegetables! Get them to SWISH the feeling about vegetables and replace it with their feeling about ice cream!

CHAPTER 5: SIBLING RIVALRY

When I was pregnant with my second child my mother in law quashed my worries about sibling rivalry by reassuring me that 'a sibling is the greatest gift you can give your child'. And so it proved, they were and are incredibly close. However, I did experience it with the arrival of my third of whom <u>both</u> the older two were very jealous! They loved their new baby sister but hated how it affected their lives on a day to day basis. Sibling rivalry is jealousy. It's not just arguing over toys, I'm talking here about fighting for your love.

If you already have a child or a step child you will probably be experiencing jealousy in the family. This is in effect a lack of rapport.

Here are some specific NLP tips to help:

1) The map is not the territory

Step into your child's shoes to see their map of the world in order to understand their feelings. For them, having been the focus of your attention, they now feel periphery and this takes some adjusting to. They are also now 'the older child' no longer the baby. You may be expecting them to be more independent, help you and not be as demanding. Is it any surprise that most of the leaders of industry are first born children?

It isn't unusual for siblings to subconsciously revert to baby-like behaviour because this replicates how they were when they had 100% of your attention.

2) You cannot 'not communicate'

Watch your body language and theirs. You might be saying all the 'right' things to reassure them but giving them eye contact, hugs and listening to them will back up what you say.

3) Embedded commands

Remember words like 'don't' tend to result in them doing just what you told them not to do. Instead, focus on what you <u>do</u> want. Notice and compliment behaviour that you want to encourage and ignore the behaviour you don't want.

Watch out for words like 'can't' eg 'I can't do that right now because I have to feed the baby'. Instead tell them when you <u>can</u> do it.

4) Look for the positive intention

Older siblings crave the attention they miss now there's a baby on the scene. They are attention seeking because they love you and want you to notice them.

5) Match for rapport

Stay in rapport with your toddler or older child by matching their internal representation and Meta programme. Your child will be able to accept getting less attention from you if when you do, you are in rapport. If they are visual tell them what you see 'I can see we're going to have some fun together this afternoon'. If they are auditory, 'Shall we listen to a story tape while I feed the baby?' or kinaesthetic 'Why don't you dance or play on the keyboard while I change baby's nappy?'